Rain Forests

ENDANGERED
PEOPLE
& PLACES

Rain Forests

BY SARA OLDFIELD

Photographs by Still Pictures

Lerner Publications Company • Minneapolis

All words that appear in **bold** are explained in the glossary that begins on page 46.

Map by European Map Graphics Ltd. Artwork by Mike Atkinson. Photographs by Still Pictures.

This edition first published in the United States in 1996 by Lerner Publications Company, 241 First Avenue North, Minneapolis, MN 55401.
Copyright © 1995 Cherrytree Press Ltd.

Library of Congress Cataloging-in-Publication Data
Oldfield, Sara.
    Rain forests / by Sara Oldfield.
      p.   cm. — (Endangered people and places)
    Includes index.
    Summary: Discusses tropical rain forests, including their flora, fauna, and indigenous peoples, as well as the activities that threaten their destruction and the consequences of that destruction.
    ISBN 0-8225-2778-2 (lib. bdg. : alk. paper)
    1. Rain forests—Juvenile literature. 2. Forests and forestry—Tropics—Juvenile literature. 3. Rain forest conservation—Juvenile literature. 4. Ethnology—Tropics.
[1. Rain forests. 2. Rain forest conservation. 3. Rain forest ecology. 4. Ecology.]
    I. Title. II. Series.
SD247.044   1996
333.75'0913—dc20   95-39685
                                                            CIP
                                                            AC

Printed in Italy by L.E.G.O. s.p.a., Vicenza
Bound in the United States of America
1 2 3 4 5 6 01 00 99 98 97 96

CONTENTS

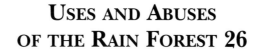

UNDERSTANDING RAIN FORESTS

Imagine a **rain forest.** The trees are very tall and densely packed together. Their leaves form a thick green ceiling that light can barely pierce through. At ground level, tangled undergrowth can make it difficult to move around.

To the people who live there, the rain forest is a friendly place. There is always something to do—hunting or fishing—and plenty to eat. The forest is home. It is also school, farm, playground, and church, all rolled into one.

Living in a rain forest is not easy. Without skills to find food, people can starve to death. But the indigenous peoples, or local inhabitants, of rain forests have developed many skills for surviving there. And since these peoples know that rain forests provide all the necessities of life, they have always treated the forests with respect.

Over the last 500 years, as people from industrialized countries have explored and colonized (settled) the world, they have introduced many changes. In their search for new resources—gold, timber, rubber, and land—they brought the modern world to the rain forests. As a result, the well-being of the rain forests along with the traditional lifeways of forest peoples are threatened.

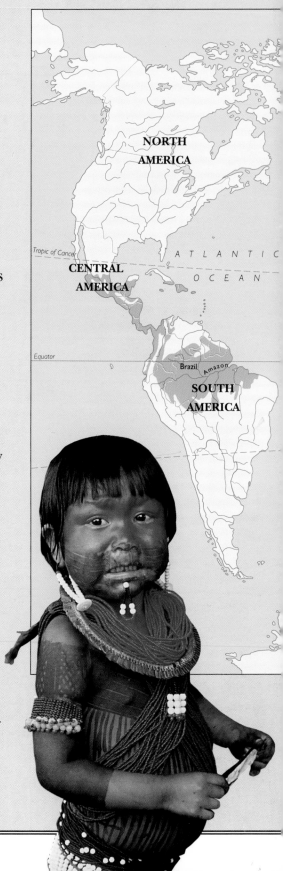

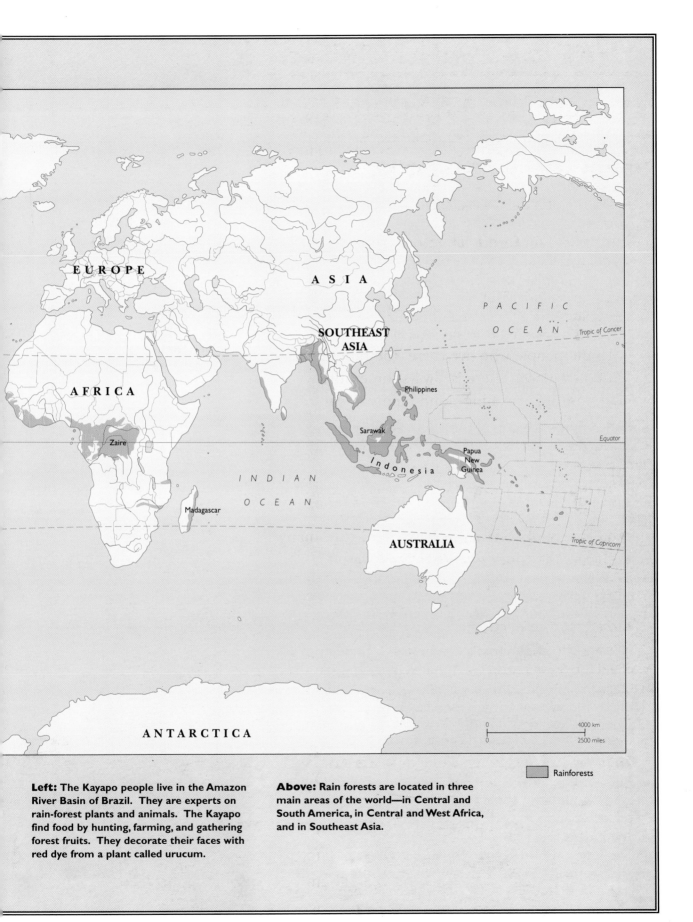

EUROPE

ASIA

SOUTHEAST
ASIA

PACIFIC

OCEAN

Tropic of Cancer

AFRICA

Philippines

Zaire

Sarawak

Papua
New
Guinea

Equator

Indonesia

INDIAN

OCEAN

Madagascar

AUSTRALIA

Tropic of Capricorn

ANTARCTICA

0   4000 km

0   2500 miles

Rainforests

Left: The Kayapo people live in the Amazon River Basin of Brazil. They are experts on rain-forest plants and animals. The Kayapo find food by hunting, farming, and gathering forest fruits. They decorate their faces with red dye from a plant called urucum.

Above: Rain forests are located in three main areas of the world—in Central and South America, in Central and West Africa, and in Southeast Asia.

WHAT IS A RAIN FOREST?

The **tropics** is a region of the earth that lies close to the equator. The climate is hot there all year long. The tropics receive more sun than areas farther to the north or to the south. Because temperatures in the tropics stay almost constant, winter and summer do not exist. The region's only seasons are a rainy season and a dry season.

Large parts of the tropics are covered with forests that receive a lot of rainfall each year. These forests are called rain forests. Tropical rain forests are among the richest habitats (environments) in the world. Altogether the lush rain forests of Africa, Central and South America, and Southeast Asia cover only six percent of the earth's surface. But the rain forests are home to about half the world's species (types) of animals and plants. Located in Brazil, the world's biggest rain forest covers 2.3 million square miles (6 million square kilometers)—an area about two thirds the size of the United States.

The Canopy

Trees in a rain forest seem to crowd each other to reach the sunlight. The crowns, or tops, of the trees form a thick, leafy layer known as the **canopy.**

The canopy is usually 100 to 130 feet (30 to 40 meters) above the ground. **Emergents,** or giant trees, soar high above the canopy. Beneath the green umbrella of the canopy is a layer of trees called the **understory.** This layer lies about 50 feet (15 m) above the forest floor. **Palms** are the most common tree at this level.

Life high in the rain-forest canopy was a mystery to outsiders for many years. Trees that are as tall as an eight-storied building are extremely difficult to climb. So scientists who wanted to study the forest roof have had to build special towers and aerial walkways. Research shows that life in the rain-forest canopy is extraordinarily rich.

A wide variety of plants are found in tree crowns. **Orchids, bromeliads,** and ferns are some of the plants that grow high up in the forest. These plants use tree branches for support. The plants in turn provide homes for all kinds of insects.

Many types of birds live in the upper layers of the forest. Tree frogs, flying lizards, bats, squirrels, and

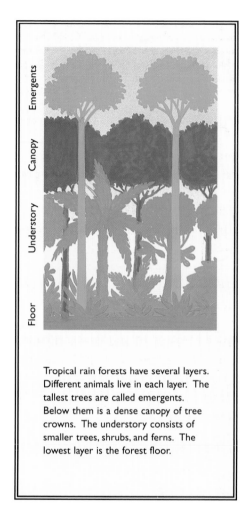

Tropical rain forests have several layers. Different animals live in each layer. The tallest trees are called emergents. Below them is a dense canopy of tree crowns. The understory consists of smaller trees, shrubs, and ferns. The lowest layer is the forest floor.

Right: The tall trees of tropical rain forests are difficult and dangerous to climb. Even people who live in the forest sometimes fall to their deaths climbing trees to collect honey, for example. Researchers who wish to study the canopy of a tropical rain forest often build aerial walkways, such as this one in Malaysia in Southeast Asia. The canopy is home to most rain-forest animals, including birds and monkeys.

monkeys are also at home in the treetops. The canopy shelters more animals than anywhere else in the forest.

The Forest Floor

Only a little light reaches the dark forest floor, where conditions are hot and damp. Moldy plants called **fungi** and tiny organisms known as **bacteria** are found on the forest floor. These life-forms help leaves and other plant materials that fall to the ground to quickly rot.

Few shrubs or flowers grow at ground level in the forest. Many of the seeds of forest plants lie dormant, or inactive, in the soil until a large tree crashes to the ground. The fallen tree then leaves a big gap in the forest canopy, allowing light to reach the forest floor. The seeds can then open, put down roots, and grow toward the sun.

The rich plant life in rain forests depends on the quick recycling of nutrients (materials that nourish living things). The soil underneath the forest cover is

often infertile because nutrients in the soil are quickly used up by growing plants. When a rain forest is logged and forest plants are removed, the thin, poor-quality soils quickly break down and are washed away by heavy tropical rains.

Primary and Secondary Forests

Undisturbed areas of forest are known as virgin forests, or **primary forests. Secondary forests** grow in areas that have been logged. Secondary forests usually have fewer species and faster growing trees. With fewer forest layers, secondary forests have floors that are more tangled than in primary forests. More shrubs, **lianas** (climbing plants), and young trees are able to grow because more light is available.

Left: The tallest trees of the Amazon rain forest in South America reach up to 200 feet (61 meters) above the ground. Many different kinds of trees are found within this forest. In just 2.5 acres (1 hectare), for example, 300 tree species have been identified. In all of North America, only 700 tree species exist!

VARIETY OF LIFE

The variety of life, or the number of different species, in an area is known as **biodiversity.** Tropical rain forests cover only about six percent of the earth's surface, but they are home to over half the world's species. This means that rain forests are very rich in biodiversity. Of all the known insects in the world, 80 percent are found in tropical forests.

Scientists believe that Central and South American forests have the greatest biodiversity, followed by the forests of Southeast Asia. Experts estimate that the rain forests of the Amazon River Basin in South America are home to more than 1 million plant and animal species.

No one knows for sure why tropical rain forests are so rich in biodiversity. One possible reason is that these forests have evolved in the same place over millions of years, allowing many different life-forms to develop. Soil conditions and a hot, wet climate also provide part of the explanation. High amounts of energy from the sun and heavy rainfall encourage lush plant growth.

Above: Most of the world's parrots live in tropical forests. This hyacinth macaw and other parrots are threatened by destruction of their forest homes. The birds are also collected to be sold as pets. As a result, only about 2,500 hyacinth macaws remain in the wild. About 100 parrot species, or one-third of the world's parrots, are at risk of extinction (dying out completely).

Below: Rain forests have many colorful plants, such as this heliconia.

Right: Tree ferns are common in rain forests. Some species do very well in secondary forests. But as primary forests are cleared, other types of tree ferns have become very rare. In some countries, the trunks of tree ferns are used to make carvings believed to have magical powers. In other places, tree ferns are chopped down to make potting soil for orchids.

Some tropical rain forests have more biodiversity than others. Areas that are especially rich in biodiversity are known as **hot spots.** Ten tropical rain-forest hot spots cover less than 1 percent of the earth's surface and make up 3.5 percent of the primary forest cover. These small areas contain more than one-fourth of all tropical forest plant species.

One hot spot is located in Colombia, South America. The rain forests of the Choco region have not been completely explored. But these forests are richer in plants than anywhere else in the world. The Choco is also very rich in birds, with more than 100 different bird species that are found nowhere else.

Above: The white uakari is found only in the rain forests of the Upper Amazon River Basin in South America. These monkeys, with their extraordinary red faces, live in troops of 50 or more. So many uakaris were hunted for food that they became rare and are now protected by law.

Interdependence

Many of the different peoples, plants, and animals that live in rain forests depend on each other for survival. For example, insects and birds help pollinate the flowers of rain-forest trees. Rain-forest fruits provide food for a wide range of peoples and animals. Left alone the rain forest is a stable **ecosystem** (environmental community). But when the balance of rain-forest biodiversity is upset, no one knows for sure what the long-term effects will be.

RAIN-FOREST RESEARCH

No one knows exactly how many different species of animals and plants exist on earth. Scientists have described and cataloged only about 1.4 million. But experts estimate that anywhere from 5 million to 30 million species probably exist. New species are being discovered almost every day in the world's tropical rain forests. Most of these are insects and plants, such as mosses, fungi, and **algae.** Scientists are also discovering new kinds of monkeys and birds. Several new monkey species, for example, have been found in forests along Brazil's Atlantic coast.

Some species live in such a small region that they may become extinct even if only a few acres of rain forest are destroyed. Scientists are not sure what the long-term result of these losses might be. Many plant species are very valuable to humans, both commercially and in terms of our standard of living. Many rain-forest plants, for example, are used to make medicines for a range of serious human diseases.

Rain-Forest Research

Not enough scientists are trained to identify tropical species. Most of the experts live outside the tropics and work in universities and research centers in the United States and Europe. They plan expeditions to the areas where more survey work is needed. Computers are making it easier to store information on the thousands of species found in the rain forests and to exchange information with experts around the world.

Much of this research depends on the knowledge that indigenous peoples have about their environment. In the past, they freely shared that knowledge with scientists. But indigenous peoples have realized that they can use their valuable information to negotiate fairer and better protection for themselves and for their forest. Nowadays scientists are expected to work with local peoples and to share the results of their work with them.

A Poison That Cures

Nowadays doctors performing certain surgical operations rely on a drug that was originally used by Amazonian Indians to poison the tips of arrows for hunting. European explorers learned of the poison—known as curare—in the 1500s. But for 200 years,

Above: A researcher catalogues and records leaf types and sizes as part of a project to study forests in Kenya, Africa. Computers make storing information on thousands of plant species much easier.

Europeans did not know where the poison came from or how it killed its victims.

Only in the 1800s did scientists begin to unravel the mysteries of curare. They discovered that the poison worked by blocking the messages sent by the brain to control muscles in the body. Without these messages, the muscles become flabby and the victim dies of suffocation.

Scientists later discovered that if the victim was allowed to breathe by artificial means, sooner or later the person would recover fully. Nowadays curare or one of its artificial substitutes is used in sensitive operations where the patient's muscles must be relaxed. The drug is also used to treat Parkinson's disease.

Above: The dense rain-forest canopy may be up to 20 feet (6 m) thick. In tropical rain forests, many of the trees are evergreens, which do not lose their leaves in winter as many trees of northern countries do. Vines and lianas scramble up the tall trees to reach the sunlight in the canopy.

Inset: Biologists in Ecuador, South America, set up a temporary research station, where they identify and record the species they find in the rain forest. Ecuador's lowland rain forests, which lie to the east of the Andes Mountains, are some of the richest and most threatened forests in the world.

CONTROLLING THE CLIMATE

Around 25 percent of all the people in the world depend on water from tropical forests. The trees and soil of the forests act as a sponge, storing much of the rainfall from tropical downpours. The trees and soil prevent water from running immediately off the land into rivers and the sea.

Rain forests are one of the most important natural storehouses of water because they grow in the wettest parts of the tropics. When the forests are cut down, the result may be water shortages in nearby areas. And heavy tropical storms can produce devastating floods when forests are no longer standing to soak up the water.

The Mirror Effect

Rain forests are like giant air conditioners, working on a global scale. The forests absorb heat from the sun because they form a dark surface. When the trees are chopped down or burned, the crops or grass that replace them are much lighter in color. Instead of absorbing heat, the light-colored vegetation reflects more of the sun's heat back into the atmosphere and raises temperatures. This is known as the **mirror effect.** The changes in temperature then affect the way air circulates in the atmosphere. This can change weather patterns thousands of miles away.

The Greenhouse Effect

Tropical rain forests act as a storehouse of a gas called **carbon dioxide.** Plants use this gas, which is present in the atmosphere, to make food. When rain forests are cut down or burned, large amounts of carbon dioxide are quickly released back into the atmosphere.

Carbon dioxide is known as a greenhouse gas because it traps the sun's heat in much the same way as the glass of a garden greenhouse does. Many scientists believe that increasing amounts of carbon dioxide in the atmosphere are causing **global warming.** These experts think that tropical **deforestation** (clearing of forests) contributes about 30 percent of the buildup of carbon dioxide. Burning oil and coal adds much of the rest. Car exhaust in Europe and the United States is one of the main causes of global warming. Some scientists have predicted that global temperatures could increase by as much as 5.5° F (3° C) by the end of the 21st century.

Above: The low-lying Maldive Islands in the Indian Ocean have an elevation of no more than 6.5 feet (2 m) above sea level. Some scientists believe that by the year 2030, global warming will have melted polar **ice caps,** and sea levels could rise by as much as 8 inches (20 centimeters). If this were to happen, parts of the Maldives and other low-lying countries would be under water.

THE MIRROR EFFECT

Radiation from the sun

Cleared forest reflects radiation into atmosphere

Rain-forest canopy absorbs radiation

Above: Dark colors naturally absorb heat from the sun, while light colors reflect the heat back into the atmosphere. The dark green of the rain-forest canopy absorbs the sun's heat. When the rain-forest cover is removed, vegetation that is much lighter in color often replaces it. The lighter color reflects the sun's heat into the atmosphere. Known as the mirror effect, this pattern can affect weather over considerable distances.

THE GREENHOUSE EFFECT

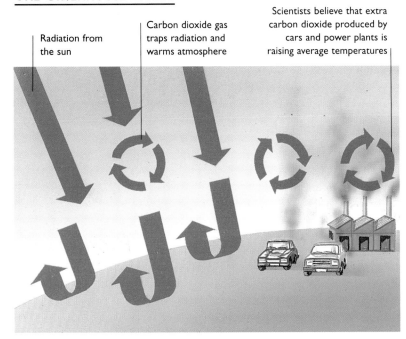

Radiation from the sun

Carbon dioxide gas traps radiation and warms atmosphere

Scientists believe that extra carbon dioxide produced by cars and power plants is raising average temperatures

Left: By trapping the sun's rays and absorbing their heat, carbon dioxide and other atmospheric gases help to keep the earth warm. Without this **greenhouse effect,** nothing could survive. But extensive deforestation, burning fossil fuels such as oil, and other activities have added to the level of carbon dioxide and other gases in the air. Scientists believe that this global warming could dramatically affect the earth's climate.

PEOPLES OF THE RAIN FORESTS

Some people think that rain forests are uninhabited, still waiting to be visited by fearless explorers. In fact, tropical rain forests have been occupied for thousands of years. Nowadays they are home to about 140 million people.

Some rain-forest people are the original indigenous inhabitants, who have lived in the same place for generations. These peoples traditionally took from the forest only what they needed in order to survive.

Traditional Knowledge

Over the centuries, indigenous peoples have built up a great store of knowledge about the precious resources of the rain forests. The Hanunoo people of the Philippines, for example, can identify 1,600 different plants in their forest. That's 400 more than scientists working in the same area can identify!

Such knowledge is combined with a strong feeling of respect for the rain forest—so strong, in fact, that strict rules help to protect the forest. Rain-forest peoples have also been excellent guardians of their environment—so good, that it is often difficult to tell that they once occupied a particular area.

Left: An Ndorobo forest dweller in Kenya, Africa, collects honey from one of his many hives. Climbing the tall trees of the rain forest in search of this highly prized food is dangerous, and a fall can be fatal. Occasionally a large tree is cut down so that honey can be collected from beehives high in the branches.

Below: The Yanomami Indians of the Orinoco River Basin in Venezuela, are South America's largest rain-forest group. They obtain their food by combining **hunting and gathering** with growing crops. Some Yanomami did not have contact with the outside world until the 1950s.

LIVING IN A RAIN FOREST

Rain forests are rich and diverse. They offer many different opportunities for humans to make a living. The simplest and oldest way is hunting and gathering, where people live off the natural resources of the forest. They hunt wild animals for meat and collect wild plants and fruits for additional food. They also rely on forest resources to make medicines and tools. Hunting and gathering affects the health of rain forests less than other human activities do.

The supply of food in rain forests is not abundant enough to support large, permanent settlements. For this reason, rain-forest communities are small. Hunter-gatherers take only what they know the forest will easily reproduce.

Customs and Beliefs

Rain-forest peoples often have special customs to make sure that useful plants and animals survive. For instance, the Tukano Indians of Brazil believe that their ancestors

Above: Burning rain forests is the quickest way of clearing land to grow crops. However, the land will soon lose its fertility, and farmers will be forced to clear even more forest.

Left: A migrant farmer in Peru clears land for crops. As populations rise, settlers need more and more land for growing crops to feed their families. But cutting into the rain forest from the outside, rather than clearing small patches within the forest, prevents the forest from regenerating.

rest along certain sections of their river, which should not be disturbed. The Tukano realize that this practice also helps preserve and restock the river's fish population, on which the people depend for some of their food. Such beliefs and customs, passed on from generation to generation, are part of the knowledge that makes survival possible in the rain forest.

Small groups of hunter-gatherers still live in all three rain-forest regions. Altogether, about 1 million people live by hunting and gathering in the tropical rain forests. But the population of most of these groups has dropped dramatically as they come into contact with the modern, industrialized world.

Cultivators

Millions of people cultivate crops within the rain forest. These people mainly live off root vegetables such as cassava. But, like the hunter-gatherers, they also fish, hunt animals, and collect wild plants. These cultivators rely on the forest to provide extra food, medicines, and other useful resources.

Cultivators cut down and burn patches of rain forest to grow their crops. When the soil is no longer fertile, they move on, leaving the forest to regenerate (grow back). This kind of farming is called **slash-and-burn agriculture,** or shifting cultivation. The technique has evolved over hundreds of years and can be a successful way of growing food in the rain forest without destroying the environment. The key, however, is not to cut down too large a patch at one time and to periodically give the forest a chance to regenerate.

Slash-and-Burn Agriculture

Settlers—new arrivals from areas outside the rain forest—often do not have these skills. Unlike traditional rain-forest farmers, the settlers do not give the forest the chance to regenerate. Instead of clearing only a small patch of land, these slash-and-burn farmers cut out broad areas of the forest.

Nowadays slash-and-burn agriculture is the main cause of rain-forest loss. Settlers are going farther into the forests of the Amazon and of Southeast Asia. When the forests are burned, ash fertilizes the soil and gives the crops a short-term boost. But within a year or two, rain washes the nutrients away, and the settlers have to cut down more rain forest. For many years, only rough grasses and weeds will be able to grow on the abandoned land.

THE AMAZON FOREST

About 140 groups live in the rain forests of Brazil. One of these groups, the Kayapo Indians, live in the area of the Xingu River of the Amazon River Basin. These people have detailed knowledge of the plants and animals of the rain forest. The Kayapo live in much the same way they have for centuries.

Below: The Campor Ashaninka Indians are hunter-gatherers in Peru's rain forest. Their way of life is being threatened by slash-and-burn farming. Researchers have calculated that in general the Campor Ashaninka spend only 18 hours each week collecting the food they need.

LAND RIGHTS

The lives of indigenous peoples of the rain forest are closely connected with their land. With legal ownership of the lands they have traditionally inhabited, these peoples can make their own decisions about their land and can protect themselves from outside threats such as illegal mining and land-grabbing. For this reason, land rights are an important factor in guaranteeing the future of the indigenous rain-forest peoples.

Governments around the world rarely have granted indigenous people control of their land. Historically many governments have thought of indigenous peoples as "backward" or "uncivilized."

But rain-forest peoples have lived on their land for centuries. They are capable of looking after themselves. They want the right to determine their own future.

Most nations in the Amazon River Basin in South America have started to recognize the indigenous people's claim to ancestral lands. But this process is slow. The Brazilian constitution, for example, does not yet recognize the right of indigenous peoples to own land.

The ancestral lands of the Yanomami straddle Brazil and Venezuela. **National parks** have been created on both sides of the border. These parks offer some protection for the Yanomami.

Skilled Farmers

The Kayapo eat the fruits, nuts, tubers, and leaves of hundreds of wild plants. They are also skilled farmers who clear patches of forest to grow crops such as maize (corn) and cassava. Cassava is a root that contains a poisonous acid. The Indians pound the root into a pulp and put it into long wicker tubes. Then they squeeze out any liquid, which carries away the acid. The dry starch that is left behind is safe to eat.

Hunting and Fishing

The Kayapo also hunt animals and fish in the rivers. They use bows with long arrows to shoot large animals,

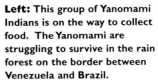

Left: This group of Yanomami Indians is on the way to collect food. The Yanomami are struggling to survive in the rain forest on the border between Venezuela and Brazil.

such as **capybaras** and tapirs. They also craft blowpipes and poisoned darts to kill birds and monkeys that live high up in the forest canopy. Fish are speared, shot with arrows, or caught in traps made from bundles of stems.

Occasionally the Kayapo cut down a large tree to collect honey from beehives high up in the branches. Felling the tree leaves a gap in the forest, where the Kayapo grow medicinal plants.

The Kayapo's way of life has been threatened by illegal settlers searching for gold in the rain forest. In addition, massive hydroelectric dams may be built on the Xingu River. These dams will harness waterpower to produce electricity for homes and businesses.

The Yanomami

The Yanomami, another Indian group of the Amazon rain forest, are the largest single group in all of the Americas to have had only limited contact with the outside world. Like the Kayapo, they provide food for their families by hunting and gathering and by practicing slash-and-burn agriculture on small plots of land. Eventually the Yanomami move on to another patch, and the forest takes over.

Yanomami gardeners use natural methods to grow their food. They plant a wide variety of crops and medicinal plants, a practice that helps to control insects and other pests.

Above: The Kayapo people shave their heads and decorate their faces. The outside world has not had much influence on their culture.

PEOPLES OF THE AFRICAN RAIN FOREST

Above: In a rain-forest village in Cameroon in western Africa, a member of a secret society known as the Epke wears a ceremonial costume made from raffia fiber.

In Africa the Mbuti Pygmies live deep in the rain forests close to the border between Zaire and Uganda. The Mbuti travel through the forest in search of prey, using bows and arrows to kill wild animals for food. The varied diet of the Mbuti also includes fat beetle grubs, caterpillars, honey, and many different forest plants. They live in simple dome-shaped huts, which they construct from bent and woven saplings covered with leaves.

Hunters and Traders

The Mbuti are skilled hunters and archers. When hunting, a group of men and their hunting dogs will spread out in a wide semicircle. They close in with cries and songs, frightening the animals toward a fixed point, where more hunters will be waiting.

To obtain things that they cannot get from the forest, the Mbuti trade with groups of forest farmers, who live a more settled life. The Mbuti offer forest meat, fish, honey, building materials, and medicinal plants. In return the villagers provide cultivated bananas, peanuts, cassava, cooking pots, **machetes,** and cloth. Historians believe that one Mbuti group called the Efe have traded with a group of shifting cultivators called the Lese for more than a thousand years. The Efe sometimes even help the Lese with gardening work such as weeding and harvesting.

Social Organization

Like all hunter-gatherers, the Mbuti travel in small bands of just a few families. The bands travel over large distances. Their territory is large because game is very scarce and the Mbuti want to make sure not to overhunt the animals. But the Mbuti rarely go hungry. The forest almost always provides something for them to eat.

The small bands of hunter-gatherers have a relaxed social order. Everyone is more or less equal, and decisions are made on a communal basis. If an argument develops, the group splits up temporarily to hunt and gather in different parts of the forest.

Above and right: The hunting and gathering way of life leaves many rain-forest dwellers with a lot of spare time. The peoples of the Central African rain forest use their leisure time for cooking, caring for children, or just smoking a pipe.

PYGMIES

The word *pygmy* comes from an ancient Greek word meaning "undersized." The word is sometimes used to describe African groups of rain-forest dwellers, who are small in size.

Since other rain-forest peoples around the world are also small in stature, some scientists believe that small size is one way people have adapted (or developed) to survive in rain-forest environments. A small body makes it easier to move through dense forest undergrowth. And people who don't weigh much can quickly and easily climb trees. Because this type of adaptation takes many thousands of years, these groups of people could be among the most ancient rain-forest inhabitants. Animal species that have adapted in a similar way to rain-forest life include the pygmy hippopotamus and the royal antelope.

RAIN FORESTS OF SOUTHEAST ASIA

Hunter-gatherers move around in small bands of two or three families. Cultivators live in slightly larger communities because their farming practices produce enough food to feed more people. They usually live in groups of related families in large compounds in the rain forest.

Longhouse Communities in Sarawak

One group of cultivators in Southeast Asia are the **longhouse communities** of Sarawak, a province of Malaysia that occupies the northern part of the island of Borneo. Their buildings can hold up to 100 families.

The houses are raised on stilts to protect the structures and the people inside from a variety of dangers, such as flooding and wild animals. People enter the longhouses through ladders and trapdoors, which can be removed at night in case of attack. Historically, raiding and feuding between neighboring groups was common. Head-hunting (cutting off and keeping the head of a dead enemy) was a traditional activity.

Families construct their homes using a **hardwood** called **belian.** They make mats and baskets from the stems of climbing palms called **rattans.** Feathers, skins, antlers, and tusks are used for decoration and for traditional rituals. Longhouse dwellers collect engkabang nuts, **resins,** and valuable timbers from the forest to sell as a source of income.

Family Groups

The basic unit of the longhouse community is known as the **bilek**—a family group including father, mother, and children. The bilek shares one compartment in the longhouse, consisting of a living room (also called bilek), a loft (sadau), a section of the roofed gallery (ruai), and an open porch (tanju).

The bilek-families farm their own fields. They hunt and gather in a particular section of the rain forest, which is owned by the longhouse as a whole. At certain

Right: A Penan woman with a child on her back carries a dish of wild boar meat. Only about 650 **nomadic peoples** of the Penan group remain in the rain forests of Sarawak. They live in temporary shelters in the forest and hunt wild pigs using blowpipes made out of palm stems.

Left: A woman of the Kenyah Dayak tribe sits inside a longhouse in Sarawak. These communal houses are built from hardwood trees. Mats and baskets are made from rattans or the stems of climbing plants.

busy times of the year, larger groups are formed to help with the sowing or harvesting of rice, the longhouse communities' main crop.

Rice Cultivation

Rice is so important to the longhouse communities that cultivating rice is considered a religious activity. Local languages have a rich and complex vocabulary for rice farming, the different kinds of rice, and the crop's characteristics.

Rice is treated with great respect. Except during normal farming activities, rice cannot be struck, abused, or treated badly. If it is, a ritual of apology and forgiveness must be performed. A good rice harvest ensures good fortune and happiness. A failed harvest is thought to mean hardship and distress.

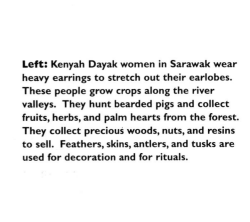

Left: Kenyah Dayak women in Sarawak wear heavy earrings to stretch out their earlobes. These people grow crops along the river valleys. They hunt bearded pigs and collect fruits, herbs, and palm hearts from the forest. They collect precious woods, nuts, and resins to sell. Feathers, skins, antlers, and tusks are used for decoration and for rituals.

Uses and Abuses

of the Forest

Nowadays rain forests cover approximately 3.3 million square miles (8.5 million square km). But rain forests once occupied almost twice the area that they do now. Deforestation is happening at a very fast rate and by a variety of methods. According to some scientists, an area of tropical forest equivalent to 100 football fields is being lost every minute.

A Threatened Way of Life

Almost all indigenous rain-forest groups are threatened in some way or other. Often their rights to traditional forest lands are not recognized—or at least not enforced—by the governments of the countries they live in. Their land is wanted for logging, agriculture, mining, or hydroelectric dams.

Without their forest lands, the lives of rain-forest peoples change dramatically. Communities that were once stable break up. Individuals become laborers, often working in the very industries that have changed or destroyed their traditional way of life.

Built up over centuries, traditional knowledge is sometimes quickly lost. Because rain-forest peoples know so much about the value of these forests, this loss affects everyone.

Above: In the parts of Brazil that border the Amazon River, land is used mainly for raising cattle. Cutting and burning natural vegetation to make pastures has led to most of the loss of rain-forest land in this region. Usually small farmers start to clear the land to grow crops for one or two years before the soil loses its fertility. Then ranchers buy the land. After five to seven years of grazing cattle, the soil is exhausted and the land is left unused.

BUILDING ROADS IN RAIN FORESTS

Building roads into tropical rain forests helps to open up the area for new settlers. This process is often the first stage in deforestation. Roads are sometimes built by logging companies searching for timber. Or roads are built so the government can gain more control over the rain forests and their inhabitants.

Satellite photographs of the Amazon rain forest show how roads contribute to deforestation. These pictures show a fishbone pattern of clearing, where the trees are cut down along the main road and along the side roads that branch out from it.

Above: The BR-364 highway runs through northwestern Brazil. Improvements to this road led to a huge increase in new settlers in the mid-1980s. In addition over five million acres (two million hectares) of rain-forest land was burned or cleared to widen the road.

The New Settlers

Settlers in rain forests are often poor people from nearby cities who have been encouraged by their governments to start a new life in the forest. The governments of Brazil and Indonesia have encouraged people to settle in the rain forests, with disastrous results. In Brazil the Polonoroeste project resettled thousands of people in the rain forest as one way to reduce overpopulation in the crowded southern part of the country. In Indonesia the Transmigration Program has settled over 1 million people from the island of Java to forests on less peopled islands.

The settlers do not have the same knowledge of the rain forest as the indigenous people do. They often do not know how to harvest resources or how to care for soils. Once the natural vegetation is removed, the fertility of the soil is quickly lost. After hardwoods have been cut, workers often are left with no way to earn money.

Above: The world's largest program to settle rain-forest areas has taken place in Indonesia. Some Indonesian islands, such as Java and Bali, are among the most crowded places on earth. The Indonesian government has encouraged people to move to the country's other islands, where they receive rain-forest land for farming. In the early 1980s, 60,000 families were moved each year. In some cases, the land where families have settled has been unsuitable for farming.

The Hamburger Connection

Rain forests are often converted to pastures for raising cattle. People in industrialized countries eat a lot of beef, especially hamburger. But ranchers need a lot of grassland to feed a herd of cattle. To meet people's appetite for meat in the U.S., ranchers need more and

Above: A bulldozer clears the way for a mountain road east of Lima, the capital of Peru, South America. With these new roads, settlers can easily travel to rain-forest areas.

How Fast Are Rain Forests Being Destroyed?

Rain forests are being destroyed more rapidly each year. Experts estimate that the rate at which tropical rain forests are being lost has increased from 28 million acres (11 million hectares) per year in 1980 to 47 million acres (19 million hectares) per year in 1990. Some countries will have no tropical rain forests left by the end of the 1900s. In Asia the countries of Thailand and the Philippines have already lost most of their rain forests. So have the Ivory Coast and Nigeria in Africa. By the end of the century, only Brazil in South America and Zaire in Africa will have large areas of rain forest left.

more land. But land in the United States is expensive.

Land in South America, however, is cheaper—even after paying workers to clear vegetation from the forests. As a result, millions of acres of virgin rain forest in Central and South America have been cleared to make room for vast cattle ranches. Costa Rica—in Central America—recently introduced new rules to prevent losing more rain forest. Experts believe that without these controls, the country would have lost 80 percent of its forest by the year 2000, mainly through converting forests to pastures.

The Cycle of Destruction

The process of deforestation usually begins with local people clearing the land. They grow crops for a couple of years until the soil is no longer fertile. Cattle ranchers then buy the land and turn it into pasture. Ranching, in turn, only lasts about 10 years before the soil is exhausted.

In fact, ranchers have a hard time making money from cattle ranching in the rain forest without some aid. Until recently the government of Brazil helped make clearing the forest profitable. Many people hope that the conversion of rain forest into pasture will now slow down.

PLANTATIONS

Large areas of rain forest have also been cleared to make way for agricultural plantations. These big farms usually produce crops known as **cash crops** to sell overseas. Governments and commercial organizations can make a lot of money if the land is used for farming on such a large scale.

Once the forests are cleared, plantation workers grow cash crops such as bananas, cocoa beans, and oranges. Most of these food items are then sold to wealthier countries. The farmers who once worked small plots of land now labor on plantations for lower wages, often barely enough to feed their families. As a result, many young people move to cities to search for better paying jobs.

The Story of Rubber

Rubber is the most widely planted cash crop in the tropics—and one of the most valuable. Rubber is made from the sticky latex, or sap, of a tree that grows in the Amazon region of South America. Long before Europeans arrived, local Indians knew the value of latex. The Indians called the rubber trees *cahuchu*, which means "weeping wood." They used the latex to make balls to play with and waterproof shoes and bottles. European settlers did not immediately realize the value of latex, but as soon as they did—in the late 1700s—they quickly began to develop the resource.

At first the settlers tapped only wild rubber trees. Indians and poor whites were forced to tap the trees. Each day they cut the bark of up to 200 trees, attached a cup to each tree, and went back later to collect the latex. The work was exhausting, and laborers received barely enough money to buy food. The long days also left no time to raise their own crops.

When the automobile was invented in the late 1800s, factories needed lots of rubber to make tires and other auto parts. The rubber industry boomed. Rain forests were cut down to make room for the first plantations. Rubber seeds were transported from Brazil to Malaysia and Indonesia, where more rubber plantations were started. The local population labored in slavelike conditions to collect the rubber. Plantation owners, known as "rubber barons," made huge fortunes. Nowadays most natural rubber is grown in the Far East.

Above: Hundreds of oil palm fruits grow in bunches at the end of long stalks of oil palm trees. The oil from these trees is used to make cooking oil, makeup, and medicinal creams and ointments.

Right: Workers on an oil palm plantation in Cameroon, Africa, live in huts. Originally from the African rain forests, the oil palm is now grown in many tropical countries.

Above: A rubber tapper collects latex from rubber trees in a plantation on Java, an island in Indonesia. Rubber barons of the Amazon region in South America lost a lot of money when plantations in Southeast Asia began to grow the crop as well. The barons also lost money because many rubber trees in the Amazon were struck by a disease called South American leaf blight.

Right: A worker collects medicinal plants in the rain forests of the Amazon region. Scientists are conducting experiments to see how effective these plants are in fighting disease.

TIMBER AND LOGGING

Wood is one of the most useful natural materials. It is used for many things, including construction and making paper products and furniture.

The most valuable timbers come from hardwood trees. These trees grow slowly and produce a hard, compact wood that is both strong and attractive. **Softwoods,** such as pine and fir trees, thrive in colder climates and grow faster. But they are not as strong as hardwoods. Some softwoods are ground into pulp for making paper.

Tropical Hardwood

Some of the best hardwood trees come from tropical rain forests. These hardwoods include teak, which is used in building boats and houses. Mahogany is used to make furniture. Nearly all tropical timber sold around the world comes from natural primary forests. Only a tiny amount of this timber is grown on plantations. As a result, many people concerned about rain forests avoid buying products made from these woods. Some countries have banned commercial logging of rain-forest trees. But logging often continues illegally.

Above: Mahogany, which is endangered in some countries, is the most heavily traded timber of South America. Mahogany is used to make doors and window frames. It is also thinly sliced to make veneers, which cover furniture made of cheaper wood.

Right: Loggers have cut trees in the Amazon region for over 300 years. Originally loggers cut down only a few trees at a time using axes. They floated the logs down major rivers to market. Nowadays loggers clear large portions of forest using big machines. New logging roads are being built deep into remote areas of forest.

Left: Nearly all the timber-rich forests of the Philippines have been logged over since the mid-1900s. Without forests to absorb rainfall, this deforestation has led to flash flooding. Thousands of forest dwellers in the Philippines have died or lost their homes because of flooding.

In the 1960s, a timber boom in the Philippines provided cheap timber. Logging companies made huge profits. Government controls on the timber industry were often ignored. Nowadays over 30 types of valuable trees are threatened with extinction in the Philippines. Logging in this Asian country may soon be totally banned.

With careful management, tropical rain forests could produce timber on a sustainable (long-term) basis. This means that for every tree that is cut down, another one is planted. But less than 1 percent of the world's tropical forests are managed in this way. During the logging process, heavy machinery often knocks down or damages trees that weren't meant to be cut. New trees are rarely planted.

THE HARDWOOD TRADE IN WEST AFRICA

The countries of West Africa have already lost most of their valuable forests. Logging began about 100 years ago in the areas near coastal ports. From there logs were shipped to European countries.

Nigeria once sold a lot of timber overseas. Nowadays the country has to buy timber from other countries because so little remains in Nigeria's forests. Ghana has also lost about 70 percent of its rain forest, and some of the most valuable timbers have become rare. Ghana now bans the international sale of timber from slow-growing hardwoods. But selling timber overseas is still very important to Ghana. Only cocoa and gold bring in more overseas income.

As the hardwoods of West Africa are used up, timber traders from Europe are turning to the rain forests of Zaire and other countries in central Africa. Some of the most popular African timbers are redwoods, also known as African mahoganies because they look like mahogany from South America.

THE SEARCH FOR MINERAL WEALTH

The land in some rain forests is rich in minerals as well as plant life. Governments and commercial organizations can make a lot of money from mining. But mining can cause damage to the environment. This threat is likely to grow as companies continue to prospect for oil and metal deposits in the Amazon River Basin and in parts of Indonesia, Papua New Guinea, and the Philippines.

The world's largest rain-forest mining operation is at Carajás in the Amazon region. Here a huge industrial site—including iron-ore mines, smelting plants, aluminum plants, and hydroelectric dams—is being built. The smelting plants, which melt mineral ores, are fueled by charcoal that is made from rain-forest trees. The Grande Carajás program will eventually take over an area of rain forest the size of Britain and France.

Plans for the mining development at Carajás include building new towns in the rain forest and starting farms

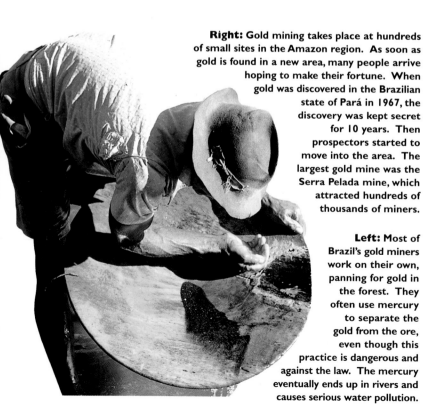

Right: Gold mining takes place at hundreds of small sites in the Amazon region. As soon as gold is found in a new area, many people arrive hoping to make their fortune. When gold was discovered in the Brazilian state of Pará in 1967, the discovery was kept secret for 10 years. Then prospectors started to move into the area. The largest gold mine was the Serra Pelada mine, which attracted hundreds of thousands of miners.

Left: Most of Brazil's gold miners work on their own, panning for gold in the forest. They often use mercury to separate the gold from the ore, even though this practice is dangerous and against the law. The mercury eventually ends up in rivers and causes serious water pollution.

and cattle ranches. So many people have moved into the area looking for a new life that slums have grown up around the development.

A Modern Gold Rush

Not all mining is done by large mining companies. In the Amazon, for example, individual miners headed onto the lands of the Yanomami Indians in the 1980s looking for gold. Many Indians lost their homes. Others died in fights or from diseases passed on by the miners. The Brazilian government decided to protect the Yanomami land by law. The gold mines in this area have been closed, but a lot of illegal mining still goes on.

Mining in Papua New Guinea

Mining is also very important in Papua New Guinea, a country of the South Pacific Ocean. Papua New Guinea has some of the world's largest copper, silver, and gold mines. Rich oil deposits have also been discovered. But mining has brought major problems, including river pollution. Harmful chemicals from the mines are carried many miles downstream and have poisoned fertile farmland along the rivers.

THE FUTURE OF RAIN FORESTS

Rain forests provide an enormous variety of useful products. An average of one out of every four medicines contains substances that come from rain-forest species. This is a tiny part of what could come from rain forests. For example, thousands of different fruit trees grow in rain forests, although fruit from only 15 of these is sold around the world.

Nowadays, though, people take natural resources from rain forests in a way that is not sustainable. Because these activities take place on such a large scale, most of them destroy the forest. If the resources of the forests were managed carefully, the rain forests could be used as a renewable resource.

Many concerned citizens are working to stop the destruction of the rain forests and the lifeways of the people who have lived there for centuries. Some rain forests can be protected in **nature reserves** or national parks. Another way to preserve forest lands outside of protected areas is to find uses for the forests that do not destroy them.

In this way, rain-forest peoples can continue to live in their forest homes, animals and plants can be saved from extinction, and the forests will continue to supply the world with useful products. But even if outsiders did not benefit at all from the rain forests, these natural regions would still be important environments worth preserving in their own right.

Below: The Amazon River Basin contains the world's largest remaining area of rain forest. But this region of rain forest is threatened, and only a small part of it is officially protected.

FOREST RESERVES

In Brazil, one idea for protecting forests has been to create special areas called **extractive reserves** in which the forests would be managed fairly and sustainably. The first extractive reserve was created in 1989. It covers 1.25 million acres (500,000 hectares) of rain forest in the Brazilian state of Acre. Other extractive reserves have also been set up in the Brazilian Amazon. By law the forest dwellers are allowed to collect nuts, rubber, and other natural products. They also decide among themselves how to care for the forests.

The change, which was not easy, brought violence.

Chico Mendes, a leader of rubber tappers in Brazil, worked for many years to try to prevent cattle ranchers from burning thousands of acres of rain forest to make new pastures. He also fought hard for creating extractive reserves. However, Mendes was shot and killed in December 1988.

Managing the Forests

People need wood for many different purposes, and tropical forests have a plentiful supply. If the forests are logged carefully and allowed to regrow, they can continue to provide timber for sale. Over time governments and timber companies could probably make more money from the forests if they were carefully managed. Once this idea is accepted, the forests are more likely to survive.

HARVESTING THE BRAZIL NUT

Brazil nuts are eaten by many people in the Amazon rain forest. They are also harvested and sold in markets in Bolivia, Brazil, and Peru. More than 50,000 tons of nuts are collected each year. All the nuts are gathered by hand from trees in the rain forest. The countries that buy the most brazil nuts are the United States, Britain, and Germany.

The Brazil nut is a perfect example of a renewable rain-forest product. Brazil nut trees can only grow in specific wilderness conditions. The flowers of the Brazil nut tree are pollinated by a special type of bee. And to mate and reproduce, this bee must be near a particular rain-forest orchid. The scent of the orchid attracts the female bees to the males for mating.

Without the bee species and the orchid on which it depends, brazil nut trees cannot produce nuts. Once the nuts are ripe, they must be cracked open by large rodents called agoutis before the nuts will germinate, or sprout.

In some parts of the Amazon, the brazil nut tree is threatened by logging because the timber of this tree is also valuable. Small areas where brazil nuts grow are being protected within extractive reserves.

Right: A family on Komba Island near Belem, Brazil, use a dugout canoe to collect the fruit of the acai palm. This fruit is used to make ice cream and beverages.

National Parks and Tourism

National parks and nature reserves cover only about five percent of all tropical rain forests. The creation of new protected areas is slowing down. Decisions about national parks and reserves are often made by government officials working in cities far away from the rain forests. In fact, the best people to protect the rain forests are often those who live in or near them. Nowadays, people who live on national park lands are not required to move. In fact, they often help manage the parks.

Korup National Park, Cameroon

Korup National Park in Cameroon, Africa, protects a very rich area of rain forest, which has never been logged. Local people used to live mainly by hunting and fishing. Now they are helping to run the park. The central area of Korup is totally protected. Only a small amount of tourism is allowed. Farmers are planting some land around the center of the rain forest. This buffer zone, where people live and work, adds an extra layer of protection to the undisturbed rain forest in the middle. Scientists are studying the wild plants of the buffer zone to see if any can be used for medicines.

Madagascar

Some areas of forest in Madagascar—an island off the east coast of Africa—are now protected. One national park in the southern part of the island is home to 12 different types of lemurs (small mammals related to monkeys) and more than 70 kinds of birds. New methods of farming are being tried out in the nearby forests to take the pressure off the land in the national park. One way to protect rain forests is to make sure local people can make a living without destroying the forests.

Sinharaja Biosphere Reserve, Sri Lanka

Most of the forests of Sri Lanka—an island off the southern tip of India—have been cleared for farming. Only small areas are now protected as reserves and national parks. The Sinharaja Biosphere Reserve protects an important area of rain forest rich in plant

Above: Korup National Park in Cameroon has the richest rain forest left in Africa. The park covers about 300,000 acres (126,000 hectares). Over 400 different kinds of trees grow there. Some of these trees, which provide valuable timber, are heavily logged in other parts of the country.

Left: The Ndian River runs through Korup National Park in Cameroon. More than 140 different kinds of fish are found in the rivers of this park. The local people are skilled in catching fish and shellfish. They use basket traps, nets, and spring-loaded fishing poles. They also make poisons from plants, such as the poison vine and akee apple, to kill the fish. Children are very good at catching small fish in shallow streams.

TOURISM

Traveling to exotic locations is very popular nowadays, and more and more people are visiting rain forests. Bird-watching tours take visitors into the remote forests of Africa, Asia, and South America. The group in the picture below is in Cameroon, Africa. Tourists are important to countries with tropical rain forests because the visitors spend money there. And their enthusiasm helps to raise money for forest conservation.

Below: Young people in Sri Lanka are encouraged to plant the rare plants they use rather than to collect them from the wild. In this way, young people are helping protect wild plants from extinction.

and bird species. Some of the plants are very useful for food, spices, and medicines. Local people have collected the forest plants for centuries. One species of palm, called kitul, is used to make a sweet candy called jaggery. This palm is one plant threatened with extinction. Scientists are now studying kitul and other threatened plants of Sinharaja so that they can understand how to save them.

SAVING THREATENED ANIMAL SPECIES

Left: Two-thirds of the world's chameleon species live in Madagascar. In fact, more than 30 species are found only on this island. Chameleons are reptiles. They can change color to match their surroundings. Frogs are the only amphibians found in Madagascar. About 140 species, mostly tree frogs, live in the rain forest. New species are still being discovered.

Right: The orangutan, a great ape of Asia, is another endangered tropical rain-forest animal. In the Malay language, orangutan means "jungle man." This ape spends its life in the trees, building nests of branches and twigs and eating leaves, fruits, and insects. Although some orangutans live in protected national parks, the animals are threatened by the destruction of their forest homes. And some countries, such as Japan and Taiwan, take orangutans and put them in zoos.

Many of the world's threatened animals live in tropical rain forests. The Sumatran rhinoceros, threatened by logging in Malaysia and Sumatra, is one of the most endangered animals in the world. Only about 500 of these creatures are left in the wild. Every time a tropical tree is logged, many tiny insects lose their home. Some may become extinct.

Over 2,500 different kinds of birds—about 30 percent of all the bird species in the world—live in tropical rain forests. As their forest habitats are destroyed, many of these birds are becoming endangered. Only 500 monkey-eating eagles remain in Asian rain forests, for example. The beautifully patterned ground-rollers, birds of Madagascar's rain forests, are rapidly disappearing. Unless the forests are saved, many species of parrots,

Below: The magnificent jaguar is the largest wild cat in South America. But this animal is extinct in most Central American countries except for Belize.

toucans, hornbills, and hummingbirds may be lost forever.

Ninety percent of all monkeys, apes, and their relatives live in the disappearing rain forests. Some can survive even after forests are logged. However, if the forests are converted into farmland and pasture, the animals are forced to move somewhere else. Protected areas provide a safe haven for some but not all threatened animals in the rain forest. Laws are also necessary to prevent people from hunting and trapping threatened species and selling them overseas.

Above: A tropical butterfly rests on a leaf.

INTERNATIONAL CARE AND CONCERN

The loss of rain forests is a global problem that can only be solved if countries work together. But different countries don't always agree on what needs to be done. However, some international agreements have been reached to help save the rain forests and to use them wisely. Often the big problem is deciding who should pay for forest conservation.

Most of the world's tropical rain forests are found in poor countries with big international debts. In the 1970s, banks encouraged tropical countries to borrow money to build dams and new roads. Bankers didn't think too much about how the countries would actually spend or pay back the money.

The cost of repaying debts is now a big burden for African and South and Central American countries. In 1990 Brazil's foreign debt was more than three times the total value of its exports (products sold overseas). With so much money to pay back, tropical countries often cannot afford to preserve their forests. Some

THE BIODIVERSITY CONVENTION

The Biodiversity Convention was signed at the Earth Summit—an international conference on the environment—in Rio de Janeiro, Brazil, in 1992. Each country that has joined this new agreement will develop a plan to protect biodiversity. The agreement will help protect rain forests.

Above: Before the Earth Summit, people around the world signed a pledge that they would help save the planet. These pledges were sent to the Earth Summit and made into the Tree of Life.

Left: In June 1992, government leaders from all over the world met in Rio de Janeiro, Brazil, to decide what new steps to take to protect the earth's environment. This historic meeting is known as the **United Nations Conference on Environment and Development (UNCED),** or the Earth Summit. People who live in tropical forests traveled to the Earth Summit to explain why they should be allowed to take care of their own forests. Forest conservation was a difficult subject to agree on because countries with tropical forests felt they were being unfairly blamed for deforestation.

conservation groups are paying part of the debts in exchange for projects to protect rain forests. These arrangements are called debt-for-nature swaps.

International Agreements

Governments of countries that do not have tropical rain forests are also helping to pay for tropical forest conservation. They provide money to teach people about the rain forests, for scientists to study the forests, and for running national parks.

Countries that buy tropical timber are also providing some money to help pay for managing tropical forests. Over 100 governments around the world are members of the **International Tropical Timber Organization (ITTO).** This organization has agreed on a "Target 2000," by which time all the tropical timber that is sold around the world will come from well-managed forests.

A few of the valuable tropical timber species are so threatened by ongoing harvesting and trade that governments have agreed to protect them through an international agreement called the **Convention on International Trade in Endangered Species (CITES).** Through this agreement, international trading of Brazilian rosewood timber is banned. Exporting an African timber known as Afrormosia is only allowed with permits. CITES also bans or controls trade of a long list of other rain-forest species, including Asian rhinos, tigers and other big cats, parrots, monkeys, and orchids.

Government officials continue to talk about new ways to save rain forests. They realize that losing rain forests is a global crisis and that action must be taken now to save the forests for the 21st century.

Glossary

algae: a large group of simple organisms, most of which live in water or in damp places on land. Some have only one cell, while others are large seaweeds.

bacteria: microscopic, single-celled organisms that break down matter and sometimes cause diseases.

belian: a species of tropical hardwood found in Southeast Asia.

bilek: the basic family group in the longhouse communities of Sarawak, Malaysia.

biodiversity: the number of species of plants and animals in an ecological community.

bromeliad: a tropical plant that grows in the rain forests of South America. Most bromeliads are "air plants," which grow on other plants and take moisture from the air.

canopy: the thick, leafy layer formed by the crowns, or tops, of rain-forest trees.

capybara: the world's largest rodent. Capybaras live on the banks of South American rivers.

carbon dioxide: one of the gases that exist naturally in the earth's atmosphere. Carbon dioxide, one of the main greenhouse gases, also is created by burning gasoline to power vehicles and by burning trees.

cash crops: crops such as coffee, cocoa beans, and fruit grown by people for sale rather than for their own use.

Convention on International Trade in Endangered Species (CITES): an international agreement to protect rare plants and animals.

deforestation: large-scale and permanent removal of trees either for timber or to clear land for farming.

ecosystem: a self-contained environment that supports a community of living things.

emergents: the tallest trees in the rain forest that grow high above the canopy.

extractive reserve: an area of rain forest reserved for the original inhabitants to harvest natural products, such as nuts and rubber, on a sustainable (long-term) basis.

fungi: Mushrooms, molds, and other living organisms that obtain food from dead plant and animal matter.

global warming: a rise in the temperature of the earth's atmosphere caused by a buildup of carbon dioxide and other gases.

greenhouse effect: the result of the sun's heat becoming trapped in the earth's atmosphere by gases in the same way that glass traps heat in a greenhouse.

hardwood: a strong, slow-growing tropical tree, such as mahogany and teak, used for building and making furniture.

hot spot: an area of a rain forest that is especially rich in biodiversity.

hunting and gathering: the traditional way of obtaining food in the rain forest by hunting wild animals for meat and collecting wild plants and fruits.

ice cap: a very thick, slow-moving mass of ice that covers large areas of a continent.

International Tropical Timber Organization (ITTO): an organization working to ensure that all tropical timber will eventually come from well-managed forests.

liana: a long, climbing plant that twists around the trunk of a rain-forest tree.

longhouse community: a group of families that live in Malaysia in houses built on stilts.

machete: a large, heavy knife used for cutting vegetation in a forest or for cutting sugarcane.

mirror effect: the process by which light-colored vegetation growing in areas of cleared rain forest reflects the sun's heat back into the atmosphere.

national parks and nature reserves: areas of land, usually in environmentally threatened areas, set aside by governments for the protection of plant and animal life.

nomadic peoples: people who have no permanent dwellings and who travel from place to place within a specific territory, often to make the best use of seasonal foods and other resources.

orchid: a flowering plant that grows in the tropics.

palm: a tropical tree or shrub, including the date palm and the oil palm. Palms have many large evergreen leaves near their tops instead of branches.

primary forest: a forest that has never been logged.

rain forest: dense forest found in tropical areas with heavy daily rainfall.

rattan: a climbing plant often used by people in Southeast Asia for making baskets and mats.

resin: a sticky gum obtained from some trees and other plants, often used in manufacturing plastics.

secondary forest: a forest that has regrown, usually with fewer plant species, after having been logged.

slash-and-burn agriculture: an agricultural plan in which farmers clear, burn, and plow land before planting crops. The crops survive for only a few seasons, and the land is then abandoned.

softwood: relatively fast-growing trees, such as pines and firs, which thrive in colder climates and are not as strong as hardwoods.

tropics: the part of the world that lies on either side of the equator and where the climate remains hot all year.

understory: a layer of the rain forest that lies between the canopy and the forest floor and consists of smaller trees, shrubs, and ferns.

United Nations Conference on Environment and Development (UNCED): an international meeting about the environment held in Rio de Janeiro, Brazil, in 1992.

Index